Alice Derry

Strangers to Their Courage

p o e m s

Louisiana State University Press
Baton Rouge

2001

Designer: Amanda McDonald Scallan
Typeface: Minion
Printer and binder: Thomson-Shore, Inc.

Library of Congress Cataloging-in-Publication Data:
Derry, Alice, 1947–
    Strangers to their courage : poems / Alice Derry.
        p.cm.
    Includes bibliographical references.
        ISBN 0-8071-2720-5 (alk. paper) — ISBN 0-8071-2721-3 (pbk. : alk. paper)
        1. German Americans—Poetry. 2. World War, 1939–1945—Germany—Poetry. 3.
Germany—Poetry. I. Title.
        PS3554.E75 S77 2001
        811'54—dc21

    2001002199

The paper in this book meets the guidelines for permanence and durability of the Committee on Production Guidelines for Book Longevity of the Council on Library Resources. ♾

Strangers to Their Courage

for Bruce and our daughter, Lisel

for Lisel Mueller

for my German family and friends

Bringt doch der Wanderer auch vom Hange des Bergrands
nicht eine Hand voll Erde ins Tal, die Allen unsägliche, sondern
ein erworbenes Wort, reines, den gelben und blaun
Enzian. . . .
Hier ist des *Säglichen* Zeit, *hier* seine Heimat.
Sprich und bekenn.
   —Rainer Rilke, Ninth Elegy

The traveler doesn't bring a handful of dirt
back to the valley from the slope at the edge of the mountains,
the very thing which can't be expressed.
No—instead, a word he's found, pure, the gold and blue
gentian. . . .
This is the time for *talking, here* is its home.
Speak and bear witness.
   —(trans. Alice Derry)

   a stranger to their courage
   as they raise a new language
   out of wreckage and evil
   and terrible knowledge. . . .
    —Lisel Mueller, "On Reading an
     Anthology of Postwar German Poetry"

Contents

Acknowledgments

With deepest thanks to Charlotte Warren and Tess Gallagher, who gave un-stintingly; thanks also to many other friends and colleagues, especially Fred and Inga, for their encouragement and support.

With thanks to the editors who first published these poems:

"Ellen" in *Stages of Twilight*, Beitenbush Books, 1986.

"After" under the name "Eveline" in *Limestone*, Spring 1986.

"Well," in *Clearwater*, Blue Begonia Press, 1997.

"Were You Blind?" in the Peninsula College *Forum*, Fall 1997, and in *Crosscurrents*, Fall 2000.

"Or the Dream?" in *Crosscurrents*, November 1999.

"Immigrant" in *Apostrophe*, Summer 1999.

"Reading the Names" in *A Writer's Harvest of Poetry*, Fall 1998.

Part I

Strangers to Their Courage

Strangers to Their Courage

Introduction

There is a certain easy solace, I fear, in labeling one crime . . . as history's "worst," one people as history's most egregious villains. It allows the rest of us . . . to be subjected to a lower standard of morality, to enjoy an easier sleep.
— Michael Blumenthal

I met my mother's cousin for the first time in a Leipzig hotel lobby behind the Iron Curtain. It was 1974; our meeting was illegal. Behind him lay two world wars and a quarter century of Communist rule in East Germany. For my part, I brought an uncertain understanding of world history, a rural, provincial childhood, and a year of study in West Germany. Only recently have I begun to understand why this event was a watershed in my life. I return to my father in 1952, the year I am five. He comes to turn out the light and say goodnight.

He is only a few years away from World War II. As commanding naval officer of a gun crew on the merchant marine Liberty ship *Marcus Daly*, he watched a number of the men he had molded to a tight fighting unit die after a kamikaze strike during the allied invasion of the Philippines in 1944. He never recovered from the shell shock; I never knew him when his hands didn't tremble. But this night I thrill, as all young children do, to attention from the parent who's rarely present. He pauses a moment, maybe he kisses us—my two brothers are sleeping in the same room—maybe he gives me those loud mouth smacks I love which tickle the back of my neck. Then, eager to show off the German he's learning for his Ph.D. exams, he says, "Gute Nacht, Tochter." This is the moment I've been waiting for. As he shuts the door, I determine that I too will learn this language.

Fifteen years later, I am in Berlin. After a year of study, I am practically fluent in the language I have hungered for, and part of me has become an ordinary German. For the most part, I'm completely unaware of what I'm doing.

3

My parents are English and Swedish; my formative girlhood years were spent in a small Montana ranch town far from any contact with the cold war. Probably my father didn't speak of the action he saw in the Pacific; certainly I wasn't paying attention if he did. Although I had begun formal German instruction in seventh grade at the hands of the local Lutheran minister, I don't remember people talking of their German heritage. Anyway, I was just taking the language. After two years of high school instruction and two in college, bearing my A's like proud wounds, I knew next to no German. If I were going to keep my promise to myself, I would have to go to Germany.

Of course I was aware of the Holocaust—I suppose no one forgets the first time reading Anne Frank's *Diary*—but I can dredge nothing from memory which tells me what opinions I might have had about Germans.

Four years after my first stay in Berlin, I began teaching high school in a small industrial city north of Chicago. By then, I had completed a master's degree in English, writing a thesis on a topic chosen by my professor, who was obsessed with his German heritage and World War II. I didn't question him—I didn't even ask him details. I made voluminous notes on Günter Grass's *Hundejahre;* I stood with Theodor Plievier's Sixth Army in *Stalingrad.* I let my professor help me conclude that the Germans—having suffered more than the Americans—had written better novels afterwards. Something like Faulkner's rise out of the defeated South. I wrote the thesis in Italy, where my first husband was stationed with the navy's Sixth Fleet, getting back to Germany as often as I could.

Since my first German class in that Illinois town contained forty students, I was given an assistant. She was the first German American I'd really ever known. During late-night confidences, she told me about the pain of growing up German in Chicago and the hatred her immigrant parents had endured after World War I. How could the experience of learning German, which I'd seen as almost holy, feel so diminished after she explained her ambiguous feelings? As recently as the spring of 1997, a German American student of mine, born about thirty years after Hitler came to power, was smeared as a Nazi by another student. Telling this story to a German American colleague, I received her answer: "I never liked to mention my last name. In fact, both parents' names came clunking down in company like guilt—even when I was a small child. And I couldn't choose German in school. Latin—that interested me." And from another: "I don't even like to hear the sound of German." And another: "We were sitting in the teachers' meeting chatting, and another guy comes up and says, 'Hey, quit talking that Nazi language.'" And another: "By the next war, Dad had changed the spelling of our name, Fischer to Fisher. We were English now."

I began to understand I had learned a language which brought with it far more than another way to talk, far more than an entrance into European art, culture, history, and customs, as French or Spanish might have done. And because I came to Germany when I was twenty, at once unsophisticated and idealistic, open and sensitive, I had not just learned a language. My first sexual experiences were with words I was hearing for the first time; my first demonstration against the war in Vietnam was at the behest of Rudi Dutschke, the young German revolutionary; my first brush with a totalitarian government was smuggling *Der Spiegel* and West German money to my friends in East Berlin. I grew up all at once—only months separated my discovery of the Impressionists (I hadn't heard of Monet until I stood before his Paris paintings) from my questioning by East German border guards—and I became that adult in German.

Before I realized the dangerous act I was committing, before I realized that I was becoming part of a contaminated language and people, I *was* part of them. Thirty years later, I continue to be hopelessly implicated. Reading countless novelists has only deepened my love of German; falling in love with Rainer Rilke's poetry, I translated it partly to reproduce for my non-German-speaking friends the fluid melody of his language. Reading Rilke forever dispels the idea that German is harsh. My growing closeness to the poet Lisel Mueller has only incriminated me further. Mueller and her family fled Hitler in the thirties, intellectual refugees, ordinary Germans who were persecuted.

Finally, I keep teaching German, keep furthering its existence and helping others love it. Teaching brings me into continuing contact with German Americans; often students study the language because they are interested in tracing their heritage. As a teacher, I first heard the stories that form many of the poems in this collection—as if somehow the openness of my ear assured the speakers they were safe. With the same naïveté which had taken me to Germany in the first place, I accepted the stories as the chronicles of human suffering they were.

An incontrovertible premise underlies this collection. I want to state it simply but clearly. Under the Nazis—and many ordinary Germans were Nazis—the Germans systematically tortured and killed millions of Jews, homosexuals, gypsies, disabled people, and dissidents. As one friend put it, over seven million horrible crimes were committed, and each crime stands separately and alone. *Ordinary Germans were often knowingly complicit in these actions.* Many objections can be legitimately raised against a book like Goldhagen's *Hitler's Willing Executioners.* However, even Fritz Stern, who writes convincingly about Goldhagen's logical failures, admits that "scholars have now established that both Germans and non-Germans knew far more far earlier about the Holocaust and the atrocities in the east than was once assumed" (Stern 136). Any other stance seems to me purely a form of denial. Novelists from Böll to Grass to Lenz had already made that complicity abundantly clear long before Goldhagen; books like Ursula Hegi's *Stones from the River* or William Heyen's *Erika* merely confirm our knowledge. The newly released Klemperer diaries present day-to-day testimony to the complicit action and the amazingly few moments of individual resistance.

After World War II, the only legitimate stance for most Germans would have been something like: *I have committed or watched committed or knew about terrible acts; I must live the rest of my life in a form of atonement.* The Niemöller confession, which Tina Rosenberg cites in her book *The Haunted Land,* is just such a stance (309). Written by the man who founded *Bekennende Kirche,* the Protestant pastors' resistance league, the confession ultimately was not widely accepted. Especially in chapter 8, Rosenberg offers an excellent discussion which shows that most Germans didn't work through or even recognize their guilt after the war. In *Tearing the Silence,* Hegi presents interview after interview with German Americans, describing how the parents of these later immigrants to the United States discussed their *own* suffering, their *own* victimization, without telling their children the whole story. Yet only to the degree to which ordinary Germans can come to terms with their own past and their parents' and grandparents' pasts by being openly honest about what really happened and living in full acceptance of it can psychic health be restored in their country. On our small planet the health of one nation is part of the health of all nations.

This lineup of facts has given Americans—and many others—permission to put Germans in the group we love to hate. We can actually say: *You deserve your suffering; you brought it on yourself.* The accusation may be true, but it is a statement few people could legitimately act on, since it is valid only for those truly free of such crimes against humanity themselves.

While the present generation of Germans—like my student under attack, born long after the war—is still often made to feel the guilt which rightly belongs to their parents or grandparents, many Americans don't see that the same accusations can be applied to them.

Here are a few other indisputable facts: world anti-Semitism reached a frenzy in the years before Hitler took power; it was alive and well in all countries, including our own, and ample documentation exists to show that the Allies knew of the Jews' suffering, and—beyond the help of a few private agencies like the Quakers—did nothing to prevent it. As Americans now know to our shame, whatever the official stance, our State Department worked secretly to keep Jewish refugees out of the U.S. (*America and the Holocaust*). What happened in Germany was not an isolated event. It is as if the Western world let the Germans act out the anti-Semitism everywhere latent. As Stern succinctly writes, "the Holocaust took place in the long night of organized bestiality" (136).

Well, only the Germans could conduct such systematic and horrible genocide, many Americans say smugly to themselves, a reason I refused to discuss the Holocaust in my German classes for many years. I saw my students using the subject as a way to bask in self-righteousness. Yet every American now living—except for a tiny percentage of our population—is living on land stolen through repeated acts of systematic humiliation and genocide. Ill will still exists between Native Americans and other Americans in the United States partly because those others have rarely taken the stance: *My forefathers have committed terrible acts; they did not atone for them. I did not commit them, but I would like to help bring about reconciliation.* In her book *Balsamroot,* Mary Clearman Blew makes clear the state of denial on the part of European pioneers entering Montana in the 1880s:

> *The country was empty when we came to it,* we were all told. In 1882 my great-grandfather would have heard that Sitting Bull had come back from Canada and surrendered the year before . . . that the Blackfeet were starving on their reservation in the north. It was a great deal of knowledge to have to suppress or justify. . . . So, when Imogene or I try to reconnect by coming back to our roots, what we find is a story that has been rewritten. (146)

Native Americans are not the only Americans for whom a lack of atonement has prevented closure. Charlotte Watson Sherman writes in

Edge Walking on the Western Rim: "A majority of African Americans have not made peace with that past. There have been no reparations, no monuments, no collective mourning processes. We can't move forward until we have this recognition happen" (92).

The psychic health of Americans also affects the rest of the world. I've often thought we Americans enjoy keeping the Nazi image alive in movie after movie precisely because watching someone else's atrocities can help us forget our own.

Rosenberg shows how surprisingly difficult the act of atonement can be when she relates how rarely East Germans who had been spied on by informers for the Stasi (East German secret police) received genuine apologies from the informers. Many informers could not get past the idea that what they had told the Stasi could not have been used to hurt anyone. Even Rosenberg, however, seems to feel that such problems may be uniquely German: "And this is perhaps the final reason the Germans accepted it—their authorities told them to, and Germans often do what they are told" (280). We need only remember how long it took the U.S. government to pay reparations for land and goods stolen when Japanese Americans were incarcerated during the war. How many ordinary American citizens protested those camps? They did what their authorities told them would be best.

I am happy to know that the Jewish woman I have been closest to in my life doesn't believe only Germans can be monsters. I thought of her when reading portions of Klemperer's diaries. Klemperer was a Dresden Jew, converted to Protestantism and married to a non-Jew. At the beginning of the Hitler debacle, he states very definitely:

> Ich empfinde eigentlich mehr Scham als Angst, Scham um Deutschland. Ich habe mich wahrhaftig immer als Deutscher gefühlt. (14)
>
> I feel more shame than fear, shame for Germany. Actually, I've always felt myself to be a German.

and later:

> Alles, was ich für *undeutsch gehalten habe,* Brutalität, Ungerechtigkeit, Heuchelei, Massensuggestion bis zur Besoffenheit, alles das floriert hier. (16, my italics)

Everything flourishes here which I've always seen as the essence of *what Germans were not:* brutality, unfairness, persecution, inflaming a crowd to the point of insanity.

Although by 1942 his feeling toward his fatherland had understandably changed, along with his definition of Germanness, he saw himself therefore as essentially homeless.

My husband and I have long discussed the reaction of other western European countries to the German atrocities. The recent massacres in the former Yugoslavia seem to us especially frightening for other Europeans because for fifty years they could use Germany a crutch—the Holocaust could only happen there. Now they see the same acts taking place a few hours' drive from their homes and are unable to put an effective stop to them.

By concentrating on the Holocaust as a single, isolated, horrific incident, we are missing the point of what we are trying to stop: the acting out of the capacity for brutality which exists in every human psyche. We must search our *own* hearts. Rather than watching Nazi movies, we need to concentrate on such volumes as *A Crack in the Wall* by Horst Krüger, which shows how common citizens were drawn in by Hitler, or the unpublished memoir of an ordinary German such as Lisel Mueller's father, Fritz Neumann, which shows how his experiences in the twenties and thirties shaped his growing resistance to the regime. A book such as Philip Hallie's *Lest Innocent Blood Be Shed* portrays the successful resistance of the tiny French village of Le Chambon-sur-Lignon. Despite their relative powerlessness, these villagers rescued many Jews.

In his discussion of the Hallie book, Patrick Henry of Whitman College cites three studies in which several hundred rescuers of Jews were interviewed. The testimony of these people provides, as Henry suggests, the model for us to emulate as we begin to fashion a world in which another Holocaust can't happen. Studies by Eva Fogelmann, Gay Block, and Malka Drucker, writes Henry, show that "on the whole, neither gender, age, nationality, education, profession, economic class, religious learning, nor political persuasion played a determining role as to who would be a rescuer"; rather, what the rescuers had in common was a childhood "in homes where love was in abundance, parents were altruistic and tolerant and children were disciplined by reason and explanation"(lecture handout). In addition, children were taught to distinguish right from wrong, think independently, and respect human differences. Regarding another study, by Oliner and Oliner, Henry notes that "not all rescuers in their study developed their altruistic tendencies from good family relationships" (lecture handout). However, "knowing whether someone was characterized by an extensive or a constricted orientation enabled us to predict who would be a rescuer or a nonrescuer in 70 percent of the individuals we studied" (Oliner qtd. in lecture handout).

These portraits are the guides we need to follow as we raise our children in love and respect, teaching them the truth of the genocide their forefathers committed and helping them live in acceptance, not denial. In addition, we need to keep in mind that, as Henry observes, "although exemplary, the rescuers were ordinary people like ourselves. To view them as heroes beyond our reach is to run the risk of becoming passive admirers, bystanders, as it were"(lecture handout). When we see them as people like ourselves, we can see ourselves as rescuers.

At one point Rosenberg comments that "not a single German was executed, sent to a concentration camp, or even severely punished in World War II for refusing to kill Jews" (341). Her statement is a bit puzzling, even if she is speaking only of Nazi soldiers. Resistance groups and rescuers were active in Germany itself, as well as in other European countries. After the Hitler regime strengthened its hold on Germany, resisters were tortured and killed. The members of the White Rose Society were all beheaded. Many members of *Bekennende Kirche* went to the camps; Dietrich Bonhoffer, for example, was hanged in a death camp for his activities against Hitler, which included an attempt to rescue Jews.

Two books by writers from the former East Germany illustrate the irony of Soviet attitudes toward Germans after the war, *Kindheitsmuster* by Christa Wolf and *Die Kaninchen von Ravensbrück* by Freya Klier. *Kindheitsmuster* details the fictional life of a child growing up in German-occupied areas now part of Poland, illustrating how her parents profited from a secure, middle-class life while ignoring what was going on about them. At the end, having lost everything, the mother and her children must join the refugees streaming west in front of the advancing Soviet army. Klier, in an attempt to understand the mentality of the lead Nazi physician, discusses the horrific medical experiments performed at Ravensbrück on young women resisters from the Polish intelligentsia. At war's end the women are released from the camp. Crippled by the procedures inflicted on them, they must nevertheless join the stream of Polish refugees walking eastward, in the opposite direction to Wolf's German refugees.

According to prevailing thought, the German refugees deserve their fate—through their blindness, they have brought the Poles to this state. But these Polish women should be helped. They resisted Hitler, were sent to the camps, and endured the unthinkable. Yet one of the survivors says in an interview:

> Es gab keine Betreuung und keine Hilfe, keine Versorgung. Eine aus unserer Gruppe hat sich bei der Stadtverwaltung gemeldet, bei der Russischen Kommandantur, and versuchte nun klarzumachen, daß wir aus einem Lager kämen . . . . Und dort sagte man ihr: "Das interessiert uns nicht, wir haben für solche Sachen jetzt keine Zeit." (qtd. in Klier 286)

> There was no help of any kind, no food, no comfort. One woman from our group went to the Russian commander and tried to make clear to him that we had been in the camps. Someone from his staff told her, "We don't care. We don't have time for such things right now."

These heroines deserved the rest of the world's thanks, celebration, and special care. Instead, fifty years of Soviet occupation (and suffering) faced them.

By now, we know that not only the Soviets but also the Western Allies took political advantage of the destruction of Germany to meet their own ends. Rosenberg convincingly details how British and American occupation governments in the west used former Nazis (basically criminals) to thwart what they considered the more imminent Red Peril. For many East Germans, atonement was impossible because their new government swept them up in the Soviet "victory." Nothing in their country changed except the name—they went from one brutal regime into the next. Klier has produced a shocking film, *Verschleppt ans Ende der Welt* (*Dragged to the Ends of the Earth*), interviewing East German women who were taken to Russian work camps after the war, living reparation. Worked, starved, and raped until they were too ill to be of use, they were released back into East German society, forbidden to speak of their mistreatment until unification could end their silence. For forty years they were made to live a lie.

I'm not making any particular case for the Germans. No one can. I don't want to. Images rise from the PBS documentary film interviewing the Schindler Jews. Nor is the suffering over, as witness the recent news coverage of Swiss bank accounts long kept secret. My point is we're all implicated; all human suffering is a part of each of us.

Why that pain touched me deeply—why I came to write the first set of poems in this collection—began the year I was part of it. Only six years after its building, I lived with the Berlin Wall for twelve months. To a girl from a small Montana town, West Berlin at first seemed endless. By the end of the year I knew the Berliners' feeling, *eingekesselt,* of being surrounded by the "enemy," trapped. This feeling only increased when I returned to Germany in 1970, via my husband's position with the Sixth Fleet in Italy. I rode a military train from Frankfurt through the East Zone to Berlin—at night, all windows blocked out, and every car under arms.

When my cousin Eveline told me her stories of the war and then described how the Wall had divided her from her father and her beloved brother, my primed imagination—unhampered by a learned hatred for Germans—could receive them as if they were my own. Like so many of her generation of women, husbandless and childless, she lacked the closeness of daily contact with family. At war's end, when crossing back and forth between the zones was relatively easy, full of daring adventure for her— not yet thirty—she made the decision to leave her brother and settle in the West. She too had suffered under the Soviets, and I think she wanted a new start.

After the Wall went up, when relations between the two countries hardened, she was also the person responsible for bringing Western medicine and food to her father and brother. She expended an enormous amount of energy supplying them with items not available in East Germany. Each package sent and each visit undertaken entailed a certain bitter tension. Eveline had a very comfortable living—all the material things she could want—but it was becoming increasingly clear that she would not have a chance to marry. Her brother, on the other hand, had his large, close family. Between brother and sister, I watched the tragedy of the division of the Germanys play itself out on a daily basis. What I lived through was not the war or the years previous to the war when Germans were doing well at the tragic cost of others, especially Jews, but the misery dealt out to ordinary citizens by the division of their families. I became a burning advocate for a united Germany, far more passionate than many West Germans I knew. I wanted my family back together.

Both Christoph Hein and Brigitte Reimann depict this tragedy of families divided by the Wall and by ideologies. The division of a country is not merely a political solution to a war, a just punishment for sins committed; it is the endless suffering of more innocent civilians.

Eveline and Hardy Horn are related to me through my grandmother's sister, Ellen, who studied music in Dresden at the turn of the century, married a minister there, bore three children—Hardy in 1910, Isa in 1911, and Eveline in 1918—and lived in Germany until her death in 1928. My relatives carry the same English blood I do. That I couldn't have known Ellen's children and grandchildren to the degree I do if I hadn't spoken German—most of them live in the former East Germany and before 1990 were not taught English in school—often makes me think the goal I set for myself at five was motivated by more than the attraction of the exotic.

My mother was the catalyst, writing to her cousin Eveline and begging her to come from Hamburg to West Berlin—no easy journey for a West German in 1967—to comfort the lonely young student trying to make her way in a strange land. On a bleak November day Eveline came to my rented room in Wilmersdorf in Berlin; nothing bleak touched our meeting. Indeed, it felt like a reunion to me, a kind of homecoming. I went to Germany without being fully aware of who Eveline's mother was. Ellen, on the other hand, seemed fully aware of me. She needed someone to visit her children—someone American, preferably a woman, to remind them of their heritage and to comfort them for her loss.

As I struggled with the intricacies of German grammar, Eveline helped me the best way she could, letting me know how I brought Ellen back to her: "My mother never knew which nouns were masculine, feminine, or neutral either." She told me how the parishioners joked over Ellen's German, but kindly—they liked it. I do picture the lovely, spirited young American offering a different and lighter perspective on those times I always imagine as grim and restricted in Germany.

Ellen brought Eveline to the United States for six months when she was five. When they left, Eveline was fluent in English. Very proud of this ability, she never lost her interest in new English words or in trying out her skills. In her favorite English story, she was buying ice cream one hot summer day when she visited the States as an adult. She went to fetch the cones, and the woman said, "Sundaes?" "No," Eveline said, "I want them today."

Believing that girls should marry and raise families, her father and stepmother prevented this gifted young woman from pursuing her education and realizing her artistic possibilities; the war sealed her fate. Like many thwarted in their search for the intellectual or artistic, Eveline focused on the material: possessions and influence. She was attracted to her American cousins who had money and power. Constantly searching for roots, both English and German, that might demonstrate our family's nobility, however remote, she often showed me a picture of some forebear who was a countess. She must have been frustrated by my lack of interest.

The Christmas I was in Berlin, I spent the holidays in the orphanage near Hamburg where Eveline worked. I slept late every day under the huge feather beds. Around ten o'clock I would slip into Eveline's private rooms, where she had left a breakfast for me and tea keeping warm under the cozy. I saw my first Christmas tree blazing with candles, my first fireworks at the New Year. During the *Bescherung,* sitting around the tree and opening presents, which we did with all the children in the home, Eveline asked me to sing some songs from my country. I knew by heart only the old cowboy songs Dad had taught us, and I belted them out while she accompanied me by ear on her guitar. It must have been quite a sight, as my husband often remarks.

From that point until her death in 1994, a friendship of nearly thirty years, we cared for each other almost like mother and daughter. When I visited her, we traveled a bit together and she showed me whatever part of Germany I was fanatic about at the time, the Nolde museum at Seebüll or Worpswede, where Rilke joined the artists' colony and married Clara Westhoff. She cooked delicacies for me, spoiled me with gifts and chocolate, and told me endlessly of her family, of times during the war, of her brother and father on the other side of the Wall.

During my year in Berlin, I tried three times to get permission to travel to Dresden and visit Eveline's brother, Hardy; three times it was denied without explanation. Under the auspices of meeting various Christians, and carrying all sorts of contraband like magazines and money, I did visit East Berlin many times that year. I felt totally invulnerable as an American citizen, a testimony to our excellent brainwashing. Once, I met Hardy's oldest daughter, Christine, in East Berlin, where she was being trained as an early childhood educator. She still remembers that I came running up to her school, barefoot, my sandals (which had torn) in my hand. No young women did such things in the German Communist society of that time.

In June of 1968, I traveled with several other students to Prague, lived a few days of the great hope blooming everywhere in the city at that time, and stopped illegally in Dresden—we had transit permission only and were not allowed to stop except at designated freeway rest areas—just so I could phone my relatives. I spoke briefly with Mechthild, Hardy's wife.

In 1974, luck made another link for me. Another German teacher at my high school north of Chicago was planning a three-week trip to southern Germany with fifteen students. When his mother became ill, the school asked me to take the students. We spent two weeks with families in the small city of Weißenburg, Bavaria, attending school. The last week, a great plum, we were to tour East Germany by bus with two other groups of students. I was finally going to *be* in East Germany, although the closest I could get to Dresden was Leipzig.

The tour week turned out to be a typical cold-war attempt by the East German travel guides to keep our students on the bus or in the hotels as much as possible, i.e., away from the populace. Cooped up and crotchety, with bad food and no place to get out on their own, the fifty students were wild and undisciplined in the hotels. The night in Leipzig they broke a glass door in the hotel—quite a deed in the crime-free Eastern state. I was becoming anxious for home, but the next morning, the hotel clerk called and said a gentleman was waiting for me in the lobby.

He was officiating at his daughter's wedding the next day. He wasn't supposed to be traveling. I wasn't supposed to be meeting anyone. I had to leave immediately for a tour of the city with my students. If I were going to get to know Hardy, I would just have to take him along. The best three hours of our relationship were spent on that tour bus. We were instantly intimates.

Although the First World War played the background to Hardy's boyhood, he didn't lose the stable force of his mother until he was eighteen. His career path was set by then; like his father he would become a pastor. For Eveline, who was only ten at the time, no such stability existed. Hardy was a fighter—a trait he inherited from his mother's English forebears. From the beginning he joined *Bekennende Kirche* and used his pulpit to preach against Hitler's evil. So charismatic was his message, he was soon barred from preaching, even from being in the area of his church. His church was closed. Undaunted, he went to the next village and began preaching from its pulpit. In 1939, he was given a choice: the army or the concentration camps. He chose the army, was sent to France, then Belgium, then Russia, in a battalion closely watched because its members had worked against Hitler in one way or another. He survived the Stalingrad winter in an infirmary, suffering from a wound, and was sent out again as a medical orderly. By 1943 he was a POW in Siberia, felling trees. In 1948, suffering from edema, he ran a high fever and would have died if a Russian woman doctor hadn't saved his life with penicillin. The Soviets sent him home. His fiancée, Mechthild Clotz, had waited for him. They were married in 1948.

Mechthild had met Hardy during his years of preaching. She was working as a local church organist, receiving her meals in a neighboring farmhouse. Hardy was so popular with the farm family that his picture decorated their bathroom mirror. She fell in love with the picture long before she met the man.

Once again preaching in the countryside near Dresden, Hardy received a request from the leadership of the Protestant Church that he stay in East Germany after the two Germanys separated and remain committed to keeping the church alive under the Communist regime. He accepted the challenge and began where he had left off ten years before—preaching vigorously against the government until his retirement in 1978.

Finally, in 1980, when restrictions were eased and I could get papers, Eveline and I went together to East Germany where I could meet the rest of my German relatives. Under heavy questioning and inspection at the border crossing, I experienced firsthand what she had undergone in her countless episodes of smuggling food and medicine to her brother. I remember clearly what I learned from bananas. Unavailable in East Germany, they were coveted. Eveline carried dozens each time she crossed. I had never been that crazy about bananas, but for ten days I couldn't have any, since the ones we had brought were for our relatives. I became ravenous for bananas.

Because of Hardy's resistance to the East German state, none of his daughters could enroll in a regular university; his son, also a minister, was educated only in the church colleges and seminaries. For his grandchildren, most of whom also refused to join the Communist youth organizations, the fall of the Wall came just in time for them to be able to set university education as a goal; the first grandchild began in the fall of 1996.

In 1989, I finally had my wish—my family together. A big moment for us cousins came when I visited again the next year: we all lounged about the Brandenburger Tor—unhindered, free of barbed wire, as free as the sunshine.

Reunification has brought its own set of problems. At a Goethe Institute Seminar that I attended in München and Leipzig in 1998, a key theme was the issue of claiming, accepting, and telling the past. Since we are the creatures most deeply entrusted with memory, that memory, like a whale's set of sound signals or a wolf's sense of the structure of its pack, must be kept in good repair if we are to survive. Fifty years after the war, East Germans must begin the process of unlearning the lie perpetuated by their Soviet occupiers that they were part of the victory against Hitler, and instead remember their complicity. In addition, many see reunification as the takeover of their state by yet another regime, this one capitalistic and fueled by materialism.

One of reunification's most painful aspects has been the tendency of West Germans to ignore and discount the forty years of the German Democratic Republic. *Oh, that was just a worthless time, a time that doesn't really count, just kind of a fantasy government. This is reality—the way the world operates.* However surreal or illegitimate such a regime may seem to outsiders (Eric Loest portrays the tension well in his epic of Leipzig from 1870 to 1980, *Völkerschlachtdenkmal*), it was the past of seventeen million people and must be recognized. Angela Krauß writes of the East German experience in her novel *Die Überfliegerin*:

17

> Zugegeben, ich weiß nicht mehr, wie die Welt zusammengesetzt ist. . . . Eines Morgens wachte ich auf an einem mir unbekannten Ort, der mit einigen vertrauten Zeichen sich stellte, als sei es der alte. . . . In Wahrheit taste ich, die Augäpfel nach oben gerollt, mit einem Stöckchen die Bordsteinkanten ab. (38)
>
> I have to admit, I don't understand how the world is put together any more. . . . One morning I woke up in a strange place, which kept giving trusted signs of being the familiar. . . . In truth, I merely feel my way with a stick along the curb, my eyes rolled back.

In the chapter entitled "Official Exorcism" in *The Haunted Land*, Tina Rosenberg discusses the trial of four East German border guards charged with shooting those who tried to flee into West Berlin. She quotes one observer at the trial: "Wessies feel they won history and can do what they want" (344).

Many East Germans remember their past as a time when friends were friends and, oppressed from above, people cared for and supported each other. Despite many material hardships, a certain feeling of security and comfort prevailed; books, for example, were prized and treasured, read many times and discussed. Authors were well known and revered. Many East Germans understandably do not see consumerism as a positive change. Learning how to deal with acquisition—and with the subsequent desire consumerism brings—has been very difficult. Once again, not just for East Germany's health, West Germany and the world must allow East Germans to value and judge their past, criticize and accommodate their present.

Natural-history writer Tim McNulty, writing of the area where we both live, discusses the early treaty policies of the U.S. government with Olympic Peninsula native tribes: "Treaty policies of the 1850s and the government schools that followed often outlawed Indian cultural practices and beliefs, and generations of Native people *became exiled from their past*" (McNulty 188, my emphasis). Everywhere the lesson repeats itself. If we are to head into a sane future, as humans we must come to terms with our past, individually and collectively. If we keep others from reconciliation with their past, we have separated them and us from healing. If we keep others from forgiveness and deny their suffering, we have denied ourselves as well.

When people ask, "Why did you study German, of all things?" I can begin now to see the answer. Ironically, I've never been able to perfect that which led me back to family and forged a new part of myself. My German will never be totally fluent. Nevertheless, it haunts me in the way the best interests in life keep us forever interested, always on the brink of new discovery. The intimate knowledge of another language gives us that brief look behind the veil which reveals humans as the sum of their language, their personalities about as big as their vocabularies. For the poet, this view is a priceless gift. Up against the wall of another language, she can see the barrier, an advantage not available to the native speaker for whom form and meaning merge and meaning is received without acknowledgment of its vessel. Forever wed to that language experience for me, the German people too will continue not so much to fascinate as to engage me, to claim part of me for their own.

Selected Bibliography

America and the Holocaust: Deceit and Indifference. Directed by Martin Ostrow. Videocassette. Shanachie Entertainment Corporation, 1994.

Andersch, Alfred. *Die Kirschen der Freiheit.* Zurich: Diogenes, 1971.

Ash, Timothy. "The Romeo File." *New Yorker,* 28 April / 5 May 1997, 162–71.

Blew, Mary Clearman. *Balsamroot.* New York: Viking, 1994.

Blumenthal, Michael. *When History Enters the House: Essays from Central Europe.* Port Angeles, Wash.: Pleasure Boat Studio, 1998.

Blumenthal, W. Michael. *The Invisible Wall: Germans and Jews: A Personal Exploration.* Washington, D.C.: Counterpoint, 1998.

Boyle, Kay. *Death of a Man.* 1936. Reprint, New York: New Directions, 1989.

Friedländer, Saul. *When Memory Comes.* New York: Avon, 1978.

Goldhagen, Daniel. *Hitler's Willing Executioners: Ordinary Germans and the Holocaust.* New York: Knopf, 1996.

Hallie, Philip. *Lest Innocent Blood Be Shed.* New York: HarperCollins, 1979.

Hegi, Ursula. *Stones from the River.* New York: Simon and Schuster, 1994.

———. *Tearing the Silence.* New York: Simon and Schuster, 1997.

Hein, Christoph. *Vom Allem Anfang An.* Berlin: Aufbau-Verlag, 1997.

Henry, Patrick. Inquiring Mind Series Lecture. Washington Commission for the Humanities. March 1997.

Heyen, William. *Erika: Poems of the Holocaust.* New York: Vanguard Press, 1984.

Houston, Jeanne Wakatsuki, and James D. Houston. *Farewell to Manzanar.* New York: Bantam, 1973.

Klemperer, Victor. *Das Tagebuch 1933–1945.* Berlin: Aufbau Taschenbuch Verlag, 1997.

Klier, Freya. *Die Kaninchen von Ravensbrück.* München: Knaur, 1994.

Krauß, Angela. *Die Überfliegerin.* Frankfurt am Main: Suhrkamp Verlag, 1996.

Krüger, Horst. *A Crack in the Wall.* New York: Fromm, 1986.

Lippi, Rosina. *Homestead.* Harrison, N.Y.: Delphinium Books, 1998.

McGeary, Johanna. "Echoes of the Holocaust." *Time,* 24 February 1997, 36–45.

McNulty, Tim. *Olympic.* New York: Houghton Mifflin, 1996.

Mueller, Lisel. *Alive Together.* Baton Rouge: Louisiana State University Press, 1996.

Müller, Melissa. *Anne Frank.* New York: Holt, 1998.

Reimann, Brigitte. *Die Geschwister.* Berlin: Aufbau Taschenbuch Verlag, 1998.

Rosenberg, Tina. *The Haunted Land.* New York: Random House, 1995.

Shabekoff, Philip. "The Followers of Red Rudi Shake Up Germany." *New York Times Magazine,* 28 April 1968, 26–8ff.

Sherman, Charlotte Watson. Biographical notes. *Edge Walking on the Western Rim.* Edited by Mayumi Tsutakawa. Seattle: Sasquatch Books, 1994.

19

Stern, Fritz. "The Goldhagen Controversy." *Foreign Affairs* 75, no. 6 (November–December 1996): 128–38.

Vesilind, Pritt. "Kaliningrad." *National Geographic,* March 1997, 110–23.

Wolf, Christa. *Kindheitsmuster.* München: Deutscher Taschenbuch Verlag, 1994.

Part II

Boundary

I. Mechthild Tells Her Story
for Hardy's wife

I dragged my bodies out of our cellar's rubble.
I carried my sister, my mother,
my father to the mass graves.

I waited.
Since I went on waking up every day,
I knew I could live without anyone.

When they sent Hardy
back from the logging camps in Siberia,
we married out of our old love.

And if he was ten years older?
And if the church asked us to stay in East Germany,
if we had to teach our children
the treason of being Christian?

They were conceived in the killing passion
which outlined each loss.
When I felt our first son move inside me
like firmness, like earth,
I walked into the cold, muddy spring,
the rubbled streets, and took my place
in the food lines.

He was stillborn.
Worse than the whole war.

But I had them—all five.
For three months I watched Christine's
every breath and held her,
not for her,

to see if I could be warm,
sleep dreamless, wake
without trembling.

When she laughed, she laughed.
Untainted. It was summer.
We wore cotton dresses, and I was young.

The children's children—
each a small light,
a way to hold on.

When Hardy got Parkinson's
he wanted heated rooms,
medicine, good food.
We were sixty-five; we could go West.
Eveline said it was my duty.

Maybe it was. He brought me back to life,
but I always think of it
as the children. Eveline doesn't know
what's asked of mothers, divided between husband
and children. Choosing one,
the other. Every moment.

I'd lived what Hardy and I
had decided. Now he wanted to change that.
Who wouldn't? He only had a few years.

If we'd gone—
then I would have stood as I stood
before my parents' bombed house—
a wall between my children and me.

He didn't like being held at the end.
He was already mostly death.
Holding hurt, the spirit
too confined.

I see my grandchildren every day.
I help my daughters.
Illness. Baptism. First grade.

I dream of my mother.
She's looking out a window,
her face lit with laughter,
trying to get a glimpse of me.

II. Hardy
for Ellen's son

You broke the law to find me.
So we could talk, I had to sneak you on our student tour bus in Leipzig.

You were healthy then.
I was young and almost beautiful.
Despite generations, wars, borders,
we spoke the same language.

Can you remember? The only day we spent together in our lives,
you told me you had already been taken twice in the night for ques-
    tioning.
"The Communists can't hold me," you laughed.

What could were our coveted pasts, rising to greet us.
You found me charming, headstrong,
like your mother. In your eyes, I saw her sister, my grandmother,
believing in me again.

Or the sun shone.
Or—like an entire European generation—
we knew our leave-taking came right after our meeting.
No silence even when we were silent.

A woman took our pictures in front of your train.
Three weeks later in the U.S. I held them like proof:
our eyes the same pale, steady blue,
our smiles those sisters' smiles.

As we walk through your art nouveau neighborhood—
mansions the Allied bombs didn't reach—
we have time, freedom to talk, but I don't ask.
I'm finally in Dresden, after a decade of trying,

but I push the pram with two of your small granddaughters,
and you take my arm—shuffling, thick of speech,
Parkinson's closing in on a body
broken thirty years before.

Not because your mind is gone. You can still talk Kant, Hegel,
the meaning of Hitler—even though your library
has given way to grandchildren and the housing shortage.
"You're retired," the family tells you.
"You don't need those books anymore."

I don't ask because here in the circle of your family
I'm afraid to put my claim on you.

Two years from now I'll say goodbye to you
in a house in West Germany and know
I won't see you again.

Why, then, are you with me so much?
Why did it seem—after those hours in Leipzig—
that we had always been together, always would be?

> Think of the sisters growing up,
> discovering each other in late adolescence,
> their long night talks, their dreams
> given to each other's keeping.
>
> One to China, the other to Germany.
> But they worked out their meeting—
> my grandmother on furlough from her mission,
> your mother permitted home after Germany's surrender.
>
> Women together
> after distance. Husbands. Pain. Children.
> No longer *potential*.
> Proven in the world.

Talk and silence,
while their children, finally fed,
played in the Maine sun.

Their pact sealed in the lighted evenings
when the lessons of the Great War still held out possibility.
They planned their next visit.

"There's a man standing here with flowers,"
the desk clerk in Leipzig said. I knew it was you, Hardy.

III. Eveline Speaks
for Hardy's sister

I didn't just hear it from them—Hardy too:
what Eveline needs is a good man.

When Mother died, I was ten.
The last month she was alive
Father made me go back to boarding school.

Mornings, in the dark, I'd practice she was dead
because I knew she'd never hold me again.

Mother and I were the impulsive ones.
When Father lectured, pounding the dinner table,
her eyes found mine.

They say he was already seeing my stepmother
while my mother coughed up the lifeblood
which had seen us through the first war.

She passed us, still the highest spirit.
My arms couldn't reach her.

When Hardy had gone as far
as any of us knew he was going,
why shouldn't I shave him each morning, clean,
what he couldn't do himself for the shaking?

Mechthild said he *had* to.
Otherwise the muscles stiffen more.
She was the wife,
but I wanted to give him everything
I couldn't give Mother.

I grieved for us all since my father didn't.
No, he said, when I wanted more schooling.
Girls should marry.

The West would have given Hardy time.

He had just laughed when Father
sent my boyfriends packing.
Later he admitted I should have had school.
He never stopped teasing me
for almost joining the Nazis.

The war over, I came West.
Every week I sent
coffee, oranges, bananas, socks.
When my stepmother died,
and glaucoma blinded my father,
I smuggled medicine over the border
sewn into the lining of my coat.

At the end of each visit,
Hardy drove with me to the city limits,
then took the streetcar home.
We were alone as we'd been when she died,
but closer. He could be part of that grief now,
let his wonderful softness—
her softness, her fineness—show.

My work was in orphanages.
Nights I longed for sons and daughters.
Then I was too old—
the blood gone, the jacket
Mother knit so closely for me: *Mother*.

Everyone's talking Gorbachev!

No one remembers the Americans didn't rape.
In the Dresden hospital I worked in after the war,
we ten young women hauled the chifforobes in front of our door
each night to keep the Russian soldiers out.
No one wants to hear it: women were raped—
by the hundreds.

The point is, Hardy came back from Siberia.
My fiancé didn't.

The point is, Hardy's family only thinks
they made it on idealism.
I was the one sending clothes for babies,
western money to buy a car and a refrigerator.
Hardy lived as long as he did
only because once he was allowed
his four weeks' visit West each year,
I got him treatment.

We had a sister too, Isa, older than Hardy.
She died of hepatitis in 1943. We weren't close.
Just this: she sued my father—
a respected Christian minister—*in court*
for the inheritance my mother left us.
He didn't have it, of course, except in money.

IV. Ellen
Ellen Ropes Horn, 1878–1928

TB dogged her whole family.
Katherine, translucent as narcissus,
sent from Maine to Arizona,
shattered in the robust sun.

Maybe that's why her father gave in,
let her choose Dresden's damp winters
to study art and language,
maybe hers is one more story

of the Ropes' defiance,
what Martin loved her for,
like the sun
a wind moves across the wall,

light and dark and light,
loosening its long hair,
her hair flooding open in his hand
which found the pins one by one.

And when finally he could not rise
above his German ways,
she still had his two daughters,
his tender son

named for her father.
In his parish her quick laugh,
her never-quite-mastered German,
made her beloved.

The War—she could discard
a country's choices and claim
the family made there.
What she never stopped wanting

were the days when his delight in her
knew no bounds.
When a country simply
had no food,

when thrift and making do
could not feed her children,
she stopped eating,
made that gesture stand for substance.

Ten days before she died,
her son carried her in his arms
so she could see the woods
one last time in spring.

If the official cause of death
was TB, that only meant
it was friend to hunger
and disbelief.

If I say history counts,
she was a sacrifice
to Germany's insanity.
But if a life counts,

hers can't be reconciled
to its waste.
Among her great-grandchildren,
one is Ellen.

She doesn't know her American family,
where her eyes found their defiance.
The border, her boundary,
holds her in.

V. After
for Eveline

Gefallen lassen
is what brings her fury,
that she has to accept
what's happened.

Spending time with her
the summer after Hardy's death, I am helpless.
She wants to shake me. Instead,
she apologizes, shows me the picture
made after her mother died,
her face a struggle between loss
and the natural roundness of the young.

After the German custom, I fill
her apartment with cut flowers.
Lilies are her favorites, but at night
their heavy perfume makes her restless.

She's not fighting the body.
She knows *its* cycle of lessening,
enriching. But she had planned
accumulation: husband, children,
house, country—where she always stops
in our endless discussion of why
her brother had to die—
in herself not metaphor
but the acting out
of a nation's grief.

What comfort is my talk
of the one Germany I know will come?
Her life is measured in days.

She fills them as best she can.
While I'm here, we tour the northern
cathedrals. She loves their solid
Romanesque. She's proud it clung here
long after the fashion was Gothic,
the style I call stone as air.

Nights I sleep near the lilies.
Each day is centered on meals. She insists
I eat: *Nimm zu! Nimm zu!*

She watches me: *Take and increase.*

VI. For Our Children

Alles vor sich zu haben
und kein Krieg im Land.
(To have their whole future
ahead of them and no war
in their country.)
    —a conversation between cousins

Hardy, I'm talking to you again,
as we talk to the dead—
not even hoping they hear us—

remembering that my stumbled German
became, while you listened,
what I needed to say—

and if I hold you
from what you need to become—
unencumbered thought
or a blitz of energy defined and focused
like the lightning show my family saw
our first night out of Berlin—

it's how we used each other
to hear the voices
of those gone from us:
I was ready to let you look past me
to find your mother again.

Die Wende, they call it, Hardy, *the turning,*
the change.

Free at last—what you dreamed of all your life
after your mother's death—
free from Hitler, from Siberia,

from dogma—
until that so-longed-for freedom
had to be satisfied
with what's free
even from longing.

No one is fooled. Life will still be hard
or harder. *Too many choices in the stores.*
We aren't prepared for this volume of plastic.
Rents will force me out of my studio.

As we crowded around Mechthild's table this summer,
ten years after my last visit,

what we celebrated
was the permission to be noisy
to talk
to move
to take on the mantle of self
and wear it wholly, even grandly.

Is it OK to work all your life
for something finally given to others?
From this viewpoint we say, *yes,*
it gave his life meaning;
he died for a purpose.

But does it pick at the back of your mind,
too late, too late,
as it did when I strolled my daughter
about the *Zwinger*'s grand layout?
The prince who dreamed it 300 years ago
later watched the sun play on his thousand windows.

At the end, Eveline tells me
when I talk of unification

coming five years too late,
he had so much pain
we could let him go gladly.

The riches we have in 1990 are our children.
Among your eighteen grandchildren,
my daughter Lisel Alice sits in the family picture,
carrying her great-grandmother's name.

She was so drawn to your granddaughter
named for your mother,
she called herself Lisel Ellen.

Or do I just imagine these two lives
unable to resist their meeting?

Or do I just want to say, you and I, Hardy,
we're still together.

Berlin, Hochsommer

Little is left of the wall
except where murals have been painted
by the lovers of freedom.

The Tränenpalast, palace of tears—
where relatives, forced to part,
waved goodbye to each other—
is empty.

Over the bridges of the Spree,
a river once divided by barbed wire
to halve a city,

over the Spree
people push baby buggies,
carry their loaded baskets of fruit,
stroll arm in arm,
talking.

We walk across too,
stop in the sunshine,
lean on the bridge railings.

History rights itself. Tyrants don't last.
Who am I to mourn the dead too long?

I surround myself with the love
of your children, with Germany's new hope.
But I miss you, there where the bridge makes its arc,
where you turned the corner
and when we reached it—breathless—
you were gone.

I miss *you*.

VII. Getting Her Story Right
for Mechthild

The way I have her tell it, her first baby
was stillborn. But he lived twelve days
in his cloak of blue skin,
the blood types battling it out.
She held him. She kissed him.

Wouldn't a clean death have been better
than the gradual unraveling of hope?
No.
Mothers sit with their ready laps, taking
every moment they can be given.

We're sitting in her sparse living room
in Dresden. Joining the West hasn't given
anyone much more. She begins talking,
telling of her parents' death
in the firebombing.

She didn't have a sister.
Neither did I.
Surrounded by brothers, we needed one.

No one in Dresden rescued their dead
and then ran. They just ran.
Or hid. Those were firebombs.
Mechthild wasn't in Dresden at all.
She was in Chemnitz, church organist.
She didn't know where either of her soldier brothers was.
She knew Hardy was in Siberia, already a year.

What she saw were the incredibly red skies.
The trains stopped running altogether then.

Two weeks before, she'd ridden the bad connections all night

to get back for her mother's birthday—
somehow scraped together her rations to bake a cake,
dragged it with her through a couple of bomb alerts.
In one shelter she dropped her precious box.

For her the miracle is that intact cake,
coming out of its box after she stole into her mother's room
at dawn and sang "Happy Birthday."
She goes back to it again and again in her story.
The cake stayed whole.

Once the news of Dresden was out,
her minister refused to let her go:
They're OK. Your parents are OK.
But she defied him,
gathered two friends,

hitchhiked on army trucks to Dresden,
in the dark knocked on a stranger's door,
asked to sleep in their hallway until light.
That's when I first saw my city—
nothing but smoke.

We started out—walking, of course—
through the rubble and small fires,
first to Gisela's house, and her parents were there,
then to Margret's—both houses on either side gone
but hers still standing—untouched.

That gave me hope to go on alone.
I met a couple friends,
but they wouldn't tell me.
Then our house—its two stories' rubble
blocking the cellar.

A school friend's father told me.
After the first attack they were still alive,
but both cellar doors were blocked.

My father was hurt, and people got him water.

But, you see, there were two attacks. What could
anyone do but flee for their own lives?

First, they just stacked bodies
in the marketplace and burned them.
They had to. There were more than Hiroshima.
Then they started the mass graves.

My friend's father had influence,
and he helped me get my bodies out—
helped me get through the paperwork,
the special permission to bury them.
He helped me bury them.

All those arrangements in a bombed city—
finding people to move the rubble,
forcing the door open—
I didn't cry. We had to move fast.

My crying was the morning I left Dresden
after Mother's birthday—all three of us crying together.
Now I hardly had time to smooth their hair.
Back in Chemnitz I didn't
know where any of my men were or how to tell them.

We're sitting over the wine
we've brought back from Prague
and I'm translating as fast and well as I can
so my husband knows too.
None of us is crying now.

This is a woman I am almost afraid to hug,
whom I would never ask to tell me this story.
She is fond of me—I know that—but she is a woman
with her life in order.

We don't weep either when she begins the story
of Hardy in the last months.
Sometimes he'd wake in the night and not know
who she was. Think she was a nurse
and ask her to leave. Be in Siberia again.

Thirty years she'd lain beside him,
the two of them their only fortress against their past,
and then he rose up calling and shouting
and didn't know her.

My German's not up to it.
How horrible—
I can say that, over and over.
You poor dear.

I looked up the one fact—35,000 civilians
killed in Dresden; 130,000 in Hiroshima.

Years ago I figured out her courage.
That's when I needed a story, and I made one.

VIII. Even So, I May Not Have Lain against You
for Eveline

I want to imagine you
pressed to your lover.
"My skin has to have natural fabrics,"
you told me more than once—
layers of silk for summer
or wool for winter
carefully bought after the war
when they were in the stores
and you had money—

I imagine them gone—down to your flesh,
on a sunny afternoon for the touching—
I mean for you,
his hands all for your taking,
the little waves of heat shimmering up,
into the body's innerness, where,
sealed off, it must otherwise be dark.

Where the warmth was missing,
you and I kept company.
After my grandmother died
I never risked again or found
someone who held me
until years later I could warm myself
at my husband's fire—
and then my child taught me
how mothers and daughters
may hold each other,
mute in bed mornings,
welded together,
arms, legs, a small hand stroking the softest
place on my ear,
while gradually speech comes.

You and I had talk—
of all the young men killed in the war
and before that your father finding not one
to his liking
and before that, your mother dying.
In your stepmother's house
her name could not be mentioned.

My grandmother slept most of her married years alone.
I never got to ask her
how that might feel
until I knew from my own life.
She took me into her smooth bed,
her namesake,
and let me lie against her transparent skin,
loosened with age,
except where arthritis had stretched it to bursting
on the hands stroking back my hair.

Maybe your brother held you
although my brothers haven't held me
because we Americans at least
have not yet found the place
between distance and incest
where warmth is.

Germany never held you,
born a year before the Versailles treaty,
growing up in Weimar,
flirting a little with the Nazis,
your brother already under watch.
The war took him from you.
East Germany kept him.

My stories stuttered out,
not even softened by language,

hacked out of the German
as far as I could get it,
never quite sure what I was saying,
the way each nuance in our childhood tongue
raises or lowers
the body's warmth.

All your life you longed for a family
of your own. Your lover, finally your lover,
too late for children. Later he loved
another woman. Later he killed himself.
In my German self, someone
more distant than my English self,
I asked you, "What's the word for virgin?"

"*Keusch*," you said, knowing you
were giving me the word. "Are you *keusch*?"
I asked. "I won't answer," you said.
I was happy then.
We were lying in your one-room apartment,
you in your bed, I on your couch.
It was summer, sweet air coming in,
lilies on the table. Like a slumber party.

The few short weeks
between your paralyzing stroke
and your November death,
I was supposed to get ready.
You couldn't move or swallow or speak.
I couldn't come to you,
sit the long hours, holding your hand, smoothing your hair.

You never took me in your arms,
never held me
crying against you.

Or I you.

Your friends tell me your eyes knew them.
Even so, I may not have lain against you,
the way I would now
against my own daughter's body,
how I hope she'll lie against mine.

My first winter in Berlin
was cold, and my small room rented
in the apartment of a widow
was heated by a coal-burning
Kackelofen I could never get the hang of,
never put in enough coal,
or started it right.
I sat evenings holding my body to it
but couldn't get warm.

You must have come for me there—
I wouldn't have found
your hotel room by myself?
I can't ask you.
What I remember is you
bursting into the room
wrapped in layers of wool and sleek fur,
your voice the first German which fell on me
like kindness.

Part III

German American

Well,

with thanks to Ursula Hegi

they let the Nazis
        give them permission

        denounce a wife
        or mother   even
as anti-Führer
let
        a son be taken
        by the Party
for care at a "hospital"

all the stories I hear
        are complex,
                intricate,
                      winding
even if the daughter's daughter is
        the one telling

        a person
could
get
lost
and forget there's always a moral

this woman I'm speaking of
her father, Spanish
her mother, Austrian
        it could have been a fruitful marriage
in 1936 the family had to leave Spain
                of course
in Austria the father wasn't
        exactly
        Aryan or quiet
and he died in an experimental camp

the mother
        the mother
                the mother
     with their daughter
both of them headed for the camps
         left that daughter with her old mother

and, as elegant, compliant maid of the rich and powerful,
         saved
           herself

the daughter
     the woman I'm speaking of,
for her it was the mother's desertion

(are we saying
     the camps would have been better
     than to lose
         her mother?)

and in 1945 took her flawless English
    to the U.S.
      six children, her marriage
          failed, she spent
       years in Mexico
    reclaiming
          her father,

proving   as it were
         her Spanish self

    the rest
         denied (she wasn't repeat wasn't a part
of that shame)

she was a girl
who lost her father

                     who lost her mother
she's at dinner
                with us tonight
       of her father's looks
                 she carries nothing

German, we'd say   guilty
      and her accent confirms it

This Path
for Jutta

Her cancer's back.
The doctors give her three years.

Their weight is on her.

She's already told me about the Third Reich:
her teacher drew her to the front of the class.
Her sloping skull and Slavic features
were an example: *Danke,Gott,*
she's got an Aryan father,
but she won't go far.

She got into the music conservatory
at Königsberg anyway, but two years later
walked with everyone else,
keeping just ahead of the Russians,
nothing in her hands.

South America. A career as a popular singer.
Marriage to a Texas oilman.
Rich. Safe.

When my great-aunt starved to death
in Germany after the first war,
her daughter was only ten.

Her early life like yours, Jutta—this path.
Violence, separation, loss
such friends to death,

it hovers now offstage,
waiting for its certain entrance,

your cancer part of the bargain
struck in that classroom before the war.

Not that we can choose our deaths,
but that someone else sealed yours,
and the world has not yet
called it murder.

Jutta, I could say Iphigenia,
a father's sacrifice
to spring his soldiers from the withering
shores of calm.

The difference is
her mother kept that death.
Agamemnon paid.

We talk. Each day is a day—
only a few can be called great,
and they are often marred.
Sleep takes them,
one weather follows the next.

You plan your brother's visit in the fall.
The paintings you'll finish.

You Call It a German Love Story
for my student Christian—he knows who he is

> *The bride was awed by the party given in her honor as she said, in Germany and
> other foreign countries, bridal, cradle or wedding showers are unheard of.*
> —newspaper story, about 1950, near Yakima, Washington

KZ—Konzentrationslager—*concentration camp*

Because she blames herself,
your grandmother won't tell you much.

Just a girl when they made her join
Hitler's Youth, the "brown shirts" she calls them.

Her father, the village doctor who spoke out,
was sent early to a KZ.

Was he killed? I ask. *Did he come back?*
That's just it. You were afraid to ask.

You go on telling our German class
the story which happened so often
we call it ordinary—
rolling toward Berlin in 1944
the Russians pressed the Germans
ahead of them in ragged streams,

the war long over before your grandmother
found her mom and brother
near the Austrian border and, destitute,
worked the late summer hay harvest.

Your grandfather was born in the Horse Heaven Hills—
the same wheat ranch where you grew up.

When he'd held death that close, that long

in the Battle of the Bulge,

his arms had to be filled with someone.

I'm the cynical voice.
You tell what happened:
he drew MP duty in southern Germany.

> On the darkened stage yellow light forms a circle.
> Your grandmother steps in, her thumb bloodied.
> She's put a pitchfork through it, and she's got
> to get to the doctor in town, curfew or no.
> She gets there. But on the way home,
> bandaged and safe, the MPs nab her.
> Your grandfather steps into the halo.
> That's why you call it a love story.

Why you're learning this language
your grandmother tried so hard to forget.

He's sent home in '46 without her.
He comes back in '48 to marry her.
He can't get her out.
He enlists the aid of his congressman.
Papers ready, she's in a car accident.
Concussion. Papers canceled.
He flies over again, moves mountains, brings her back.
Steamer across the Atlantic. Bus across the U.S.

And what did she think then,
with her husband's Danish name,
the good English she learned from her father,
to save her?

My grandfather's family was respected in that town, you say.
My grandmother didn't have any trouble.

> Just scared—as she took up the life of the wheat rancher

in his brown hill country. When spring brought the wheat,
its green too-glittery bands taunted her
with the goodbye hug from her father,

while she marched with the young girls in white,
tossing bouquets to the Führer
like a trigger to the head she loved.

Immigrant

Because you're her mother,
you give her
every moment
to say words
you will never say
instinctively, much less well—
I mean the long worsted sentences
one speaks to children,
even to babies,
wrapping them in a cocoon
they will find their way out of
flying.

You're making sure
she will reach smoothly the accents
which will make her
part of this country
since that's why your husband
has brought you here,
for the sake of your children.

She merely endures
the tongue *your* mouth
knows by heart,
slipping into tiny cracks
and sampling each morsel
of existence,
while the one you speak to her
in front of her friends' mothers
comes off in your hands
in large clots
and sharp-edged bits,
as if you buried her in them
rather than wrapped her
in the comforter

she could grow warm in.

You're the one
helping her grow away
from what you might say to her,
and the place her new words take her
is a place you've never been,
not the one
you had prepared all along.

Your heart's in the old country.
That talk's your skin,
holding all the parts together,
not this wad
you can't get your mouth around.

When you try,
she's only embarrassed.
Mother, please,
we don't talk that way here.

Jackboots

a woman talks to me after a presentation in my German class

Why shouldn't we
have welcomed them?
For years the Czechs had crowded us,
refused to learn German.
We were Sudetenland coming home.

Until '42 when we couldn't
get our winter's coal,
and every night was blackout.

Until '42 I'm sure my folks
didn't know about the camps.
When I asked my dad what Aryan meant,
he said pure German blood.
When I asked what the difference
between us and Jews was,
he said, "Honey, there really isn't anything."

I turned ten and had to wear the blue skirt and white blouse
of Hitler's youth—had to collect old paper,
people's silver,
all for the Reich.

We gave our brother. In the Crimea
in 1944. We won't ever know
if he was buried.

And when the flood of refugees
began, we gave clothes,
food, a place to sleep,
even our suitcases.
With our two-story house in the country
and Dad's wages, we figured we were safe.

We weren't. The Russians
came without any rules.
Once, a soldier rushed into the yard,
turned on our outdoor tap
and watched the water flow.

He'd never seen a faucet.

He cut it loose with his machete,
took it over to a brick wall
and tried to turn the water on.
When none came out,
he turned his machete on us.

I didn't tell the class my sisters
and I lived all summer
hidden in our attic.
The soldiers raped everyone
they could.

By fall, a different regiment,
soldiers quartered in our house.
They didn't stop the starving.
Twelve and thirteen, my sister and I
blackened our faces,
defied curfew and hunted nights
for potatoes, cabbages, apples.

Maybe that's why Ilse, my brother's twin,
tried to escape to the Americans—
one person less to feed.
Soldiers picked her up,
sent her to Siberia.

The Russians needed my dad
to get the city running—electricity,
railroads, bridges. They worked him

—in the grip of pneumonia—
right to the edge of death.

Then, in a sudden moment of what? mercy?
that one barged into our house at Christmas,
bringing bread and sausage.
He saved us.

Spring, they got rid of us—
clothes on our backs and wedding rings.
Thirty cattle cars, fifty to a car.
No food in Bavaria either, and no one wanted us.
Out from the old farmhouse
forced to take us in
we picked mushrooms, gathered a little wood,
hitchhiked thirty miles to München
to barter for flour.

We lost everything
our family had had for hundreds of years,
but we got Ilse back,
head shaved,
covered with boils,
dysentery.

We got Ilse back.

Or the Dream?

Is the beginning
    both his hands blown off
    on the Russian front?

Or the dream his daughter
    dreams fifty years later
    in her warm farmhouse in the U.S.,
    finding herself once more
    on her belly in the ditch,
    forcing her breath slow,
    her heartbeat slow,
    until the French guards pass by?

Or is the beginning
    her mother
    whose first conscious thought
    already contained Hitler?
    At sixteen, she was asked,
    Munitions factory or nurse?
    OK, she said, nurse.
    Six weeks training
    and they began pouring
    into her ward—

Burns. The most unimaginable
    parts gone.
    His hands.

So they are, then, the beginning?
    Or the questions?
    How could he reach up to her?
    How could he begin to caress her?
    How could she marry him?

Or is it the great silence

in which their daughter grew?
Ten years of French occupation.
No one explained
why the French were paying them back
with starvation.

On the farms
   cows raised in cellars,
   misshapen cows who never
   saw light or walked
   a pasture,
   but ate and were butchered.

No one talked,
   but the daughter learned
   Kristallnacht, Jews beat up.
   In this town of 5,000,
   forty taken—not Jews—
   children.

If a child had red hair—
   sure sign of incest—
   if he were slow
   or she crippled—

The authorities came. Your child
   was given a vacation.
   Maybe they were
   the beginning.

In a few weeks, ashes
   returned to you. Your child
   had had an accident.
   Soon you could guess when
   they would knock on your door.
   Vacations could not be refused.

Is it, then, the children?

Stealing was their daughter's way of life.
If children stole,
the French guards would only kick them
or rough them up.
They could keep the food.

Her grandfather was imprisoned
    five years
    for shooting a wild boar,
    but they saved the meat,
    buried under the sheets of a laundry basket.

After the French left,
    their daughter married
    an American.

Is it, yes, the silence children breathe in,
    where nothing is ever said,
    but they are listening,

and the tiny granddaughter asks,
    Did Grandpa Joe shoot
    Grandpa Friedrich's hands off?

Small Gifts of Fruit

After the war
in the starvation time
the small gifts

of fruit and flour,
powdered milk,
arrived on her family's doorstep.

The only ones who had food
were those the Nazis
had tried to starve:

Jews. Dissidents.
The Allies began
to fortify them.

Since her father's dead now,
she can't ask
how he managed.

True, he was in charge
of many workers,
but above him, after all,

his own bosses.
How did he stay out of the party,
keep half-Jews,

socialists,
working quietly
in the firm?

Their silent packets.
These kept
her family going.

He Grew Up West of Innsbruck

In the bundle we all carry from childhood,
his contained this:

His father, S.A., S.S., Stalingrad, Siberia.
His father's last letter to him came in '53.

Fathers gone, fourteen cousins
and their mothers lived in one house.

He was six that day at the dentist's. Sirens.
B-17s all over. Four days before he got home.

Starvation began in the winter of '44.
'45, '46, '47. They stayed alive on dogfood.

His grandfather stole it at the officers' club.
He remembers being full about once a week.

When the Russians came, an aunt and uncle
were rolled away in the boxcars. No letters at all.

Neither his father nor his mother "knew about the camps."
They knew their Jewish neighbor, knew his Protestant wife

who wouldn't sign papers for their two sons in the S.S.
The sons never returned.

Under the fluorescent lights of my classroom, all eyes
on him, he's struggling to untie the knots.

He's brought his grandfather's helmet
from World War I, brigadier general,

and he holds what it should mean
with what history has made clear to him,

whatever of Austria was handed to Italy in 1919,
things went way beyond payback.

As he works his sweaty wad of stories, students begin
to ask, "Why wouldn't she sign the papers?"

"How old were the sons?" He's still his skinny self
fighting with cousins over dogfood.

"My uncles smuggled people into Switzerland."
"My aunt married a Jew and saved him from Dachau,"

he recites, and it's not exactly that he thinks
they haven't accepted his justification.

He's not really listening, possibility being
the bright flame of hope, fact, its abandonment.

His father didn't crawl back. His body
wasn't returned—the place where grief is.

His mother could cross into his stepfather's shadow.
For him, the ceaseless running ahead,

days withdrawing into the future
like perspective in the paintings of the 1400s.

Illusion. He wakes and sleeps and wakes for months,
years even, then watches a man

lift his small son into a car and feels that stretch
underneath the arms, careless closeness.

The hour is over. Carefully he folds his bundle.
He's the one who has to carry it.

Two Sisters: Some Remnants

Hilde

This is my father holding me.
Here, Elske and I in our wading pool, and he's sitting with us.
See, even here, he's got the uniform on.

I found it in the album long after the war.
In adolescence, I suppose. Because I don't remember the uniform.
I know now he was a Nazi.

I'm sure that's why he stayed for the last Russian siege
of our town. So he'd be killed.
Of course, it was one's duty to fight to the end.
That's why he *could* stay.
But he had enough connections to get our family out.

Going on is left to women.
Mother had a brother in Erfurt.
She took us there, two sons and two daughters,
five of us with nothing but ourselves.
We lived on his charity in one room.
Mother learned to be a secretary.

Father was good and kind.
I'm past the age where I need to be loyal.
If he hadn't been kind, I could say it.

Maybe I was too young.
But his hands holding me feel gentle.
He never raised his voice.
What I remember from the pool picture is sun.
He kept us safe: nothing came into those days.

Of course. He was a Nazi.

Elske

Let's start at the Dom Platz—the cathedral
with its famous bell, *Maria Gloriosa.*

The steps lead down into the heart of the city,
Erfurt, where I was a girl—until '56
when my brothers were in so much trouble with the government,
my mother got us all out.

No one realized at first how the Communists would be.
We kept waiting, thinking, OK, after such and such,
things will get better.

They didn't. Stuttgart. I studied in Tübingen. Came to the U.S.
Once you're afloat, what's the difference?

So this summer when Hilde got me back—she said I had
to come now the East was open—
I hadn't seen Erfurt in 35 years. It's one thing to grow up someplace
and leave and go back or not, as you feel you must or can't.
The land's there and you choose it or you don't.
The part that's in you is in you anyway.
I mean the imprint—how the land gave you itself
until you're always giving it back with every word and gesture.

But when your city's taken from you by force
and you think you can never get back,
your connection is always sharpened
by a little hysteria and a kind of despair—
protected too, you know—packaged and laid on a shelf.
You don't get finished. No way to see things again
with different eyes.

The wheat fields stretching all those miles around the city.
As Hilde drove through them, I just let the tears run.

We went to Mother's grave.

I never heard Mother talk about anything but practical matters.
If she missed my father, if she hated the Nazis but loved him anyway,
if she cringed at the humiliation her brother offered,
if she saw herself always further from home—
East Prussia went to Poland—she didn't tell us.
She got us schooling.

Another day, the marketplace.
People selling things as always—
100 large bras—all the same size and style—
hung up to fly in the breeze.
We waded through them to get inside.

Hilde began to chat—she always does—
the shop woman knew my mother; other people came in,
and yes, they knew our family. I was back where I'd been—
eight or nine again, there with Mother.
Everything hanging in the air but nothing spoken—
except the birthday gift we'd come for.

Hilde planned an itinerary.
The day for Buchenwald got lost in a flea market.
Other days squandered on our elementary school,
our uncle's house.
Only the luck of the draw that his stood and ours didn't,
but he let my mother know her life was tainted.

I used to say, that's behind me. I didn't build the Wall.
My life was in Spokane with my husband and two sons.
Alcohol, other women. I raised the boys alone—
just like Mother.

Hilde's house was built in 1750.
She'll probably lose it because her husband's
left her too, and she can't find work.
The ground floor is one thing, but upstairs—
a tangle of boxes, clothes, books, dust.
Every day she talked about getting to it.

The third floor—the attic—her husband refinished
in pine and skylights. It's cool, empty.

Hilde and I get migraines. Something wants out.
I was with her a month. Back in Spokane, six.
Lonely without Hilde. Lonely with her.

Were You Blind?

Yes, you said, *yes,*
I was, after my stroke.
But some of my sight's back now.

The story you're telling my class
happened fifty years before the stroke. You almost
turned your father in for listening to the BBC.

Before that, when you were nine,
the Nazis evacuated you from Bremen.
You were leaving your mother for the first time.

The narrow gauge stopped deep in the Harz
far from the reach of British bombers.
You got out with your suitcase.

Families were grabbing children—
free labor from the *lieber Führer.*
An old couple headed off with you.

Just one crippled boy left on the Bahnsteig
when a man rushed up, late,
and forced you from the old people.

You were glad until you found out
the couple owned a toy store.
The crippled boy had some great times.

Your house was the city florist,
greedy with wreaths for the dead.
This woman—your new mother.

She asked the question which makes
all the rest easy. *Couldn't you find*
a bigger one? He can't work.

But you did. You worked in the flower fields
with Edouard, the French POW,
also a gift to the florist.

The Red Cross brought him news
of his son's birth and small packages from home.
He shared the chocolate with you.

Then, like a father, with the little German he had,
he taught you how to survive from the earth—
which plants, finding snails, snaring birds.

You show the class how to make the bird trap.
He was the only one who cared about me,
and he wasn't blond or blue-eyed.

That was how, you see, I learned
my lesson, about the master race.
Even if I was still part of the Hitler Youth.

Three years later, taken from the florist's,
your job was to stand at the Bahnhof,
feeding refugees soup as the trains brought them West.

One day cars on the other track.
You watched someone try to wedge an arm out,
reach down and scoop up a little of the urine-soaked snow.

Shouldn't you give them something?
Hardened criminals, they told you,
the really bad ones.

I believed them. They wore the striped uniforms.
That was the only time I saw Juden.
That was enough.

'45, back in Bremen, ready to turn

your father in. Remnants of defeated Wehrmacht
roamed the bombed streets,

their Mausers making sport, picking off Brits.
The war was over. I was scared.
I saw Edouard's face in every man they mowed down.

"Well, If That's What You Lived Through . . ."
our waiter to an elderly customer

—the European custom is to use both both fork and knife when eating.

Is he drunk?
No matter what—
the elderly man at the bar
has to tell his story.
He's pestering our waiter,
who's trying hard to listen.

Half a century,
but he can't get free of his picture
of how the Jews from this town
were loaded up and taken away.
He still knows exactly—
and he points with his outstretched arms—
men left, women and children right.

My daughter and I are seeing each other
for the first time since her German course for children
began three weeks ago.
This afternoon in our third-story room
of this not-quite-shabby family hotel,
under the slanting roof,
after talking we began again and again,
we took a nap. For the first time since we'd parted,
I slept deeply without dreaming.

She's learning fast.
She knows to take her fork in her left hand,
her knife in her right.
"It looks good," she tells me.

Everyone in the restaurant
can tell we're Americans—

the ones who freed them, occupied them,
were there.
At every table dead silence
while the man insists
the waiter hear his story.

"This is an interesting story,"
I whisper to my daughter,
but her mind is on how long
we've been apart—she wants to talk,
wants me to cut our Schnitzel into small pieces,
wants to call the waiter for ketchup and water.
It's our day of reunion.

"So," the waiter says to the man
as soon as he's come to us
and also delivered a beer to the table across,
"so no one came back."
"No," says the man,
and after a bit, he pays and goes.

I'm ready to pay too,
but first I want to talk a little with our patient waiter
who has spoken English
with my daughter.

He's spent time in other countries,
in Switzerland at the Matterhorn.
"Then the English words were always
first on my tongue," he says.
"They've retreated a bit now."

"And how did you like the Matterhorn?"

"Whatever the Swiss bellow about neutrality,
they hate foreigners too.
And when you've reached two times twenty
and then some, I'd rather be back home."

His talk is soft, a bit girlish.
After he takes our money,
I watch his walk back to the bar.
I'm sure he could hear
the story of the Jews thousands of times.

My daughter and I sleep warm
under the feather beds of this spa town—
where I've let young, friendly,
able Germans
teach her their language.
It's what we both want.

Look, the picture I took away from Dachau
is titled *A Mother Goes with Her Children to the Gas Chamber.*
She's going,
but her curved body shows
how she shields them—it's clear—
protects them. That's what mothers are for.
She's carrying her baby. The other two
hold tight to her black skirt.
She can't hurry. She can't.

And from the elderly customer,
his walk out into the old town
where the restored Fachwerk gleams.

"OK," I say to my daughter. "Shall
we go?"
"Let's go," she says. "Let's go."

Herself a Daughter

The daughter's past 50 herself,
but in the story she's telling me—
even as I move away from her—
her mother is 17,
herself a daughter,
fighting with her father
when the sirens sound,
and they run for the cellar.
She can't fight him with words
since she doesn't want to be hit,
so in defiance she slams out the cellar door.
As it wallops against its jamb,
she hears the bomb thud,
killing her father, mother, brothers.
By 18 she's delivering—
her teeth clenched against the sheet they gave her—
an American's spoil of war.
He doesn't want his daughter—
the woman telling me this story—
and neither does her mother,
so she's left five years
with a great-aunt who, childless,
lights somewhere in the after-war devastation
and loves this baby like her own.

The mother, finding at last the American husband
who does want her,
comes back for her daughter
and that's when it begins,
living with a woman
who hears the crash of a door
the thud of a bomb
and loses in the instant
her right,
her only means,

not to be raped
or loved
or whatever that first GI did,
the thud of a door, a bomb
and the cry of a child
the thud of a door a bomb
herself
her father
this man above her
in the nights.

Whether He Was Still Running West

Königsberg, capital city of German East Prussia for 700 years, became part of the Soviet Union after World War II.

Well, yes, I am German American,
he admitted after I asked directly
in the long onslaught of our talk on school matters.

His family schlepped out of Königsberg
and dropped in East Germany,
where starvation pressed his mother down.
No word from his father in Siberia.
She kept her daughter and gave her two sons, four and three,
to the Communists to raise.
Seven years in the orphanage and the Communists—
resourceless after all—turned the boys back to their grandparents.

In 1953, when I was 11, during the uprising,
our grandfather took us to the border at Halle.
Your chance, he said. I can't leave your grandmother.
Run for it. They did, running through fields
and then woods. He didn't even know
whether he was still running west, Jakob's hand
clutched like death to his, nothing in his lungs,
one shoe down, then the other,
the years passing over him:
how he'd clung to his mother letting him go—
hunger like a friend he'd lost interest in but couldn't get rid of—
his grandmother, another stranger.
The pound of their feet on pavement,
narrowly missed by a car, border police finally stopping them,
the refugee camp in the West—once more *other.*

During high school, I got my chance to come to the U.S.,
and I found a way to stay.
Sometimes I do visit. My mom tells me
what a happy boy I was—even now, Du hast so ein sonniges

Gemüt. After a couple weeks, they rub me
the wrong way. Really, Germans are so morbid.

Wouldn't you love your children equally?
Wouldn't you rather starve together
than give them to strangers?
Or does that only seem true,
if—like me—your toddlers
aren't hungry and calling out to you?
Did you think, here at least they'll be fed?
Or did you just give up and give in
to the Communist line about how
they could raise your children better?
Or had you already given up,
not really wanting more children after your daughter,
but for your husband's sake,
who wasn't coming back now
to raise those boys?
Or just the piercing missing of him
gone so long from the sweet bed of your lovemaking?
Or the years growing up in a house on stolen land—
although your parents didn't say it—
and the widening silence after you were ten
with a government they didn't really believe in
but which kept order and gave *Lebensraum*?
And then it was too late—you had to be part of it or die,
your choices:
choose death or choose death.

You chose death
and gave your children up.

No Way but Forward

On December 6, Knecht Ruprecht accompanies St. Nikolaus on his rounds and hands out switches to naughty children.

There is the bread, yes,
but the case too, the small plastic case
which snapped shut, holding its toothbrush
and a bright yellow washcloth secure.
Just as her eyes hold it out to us now,
a GI placed it in her hands. First grade.
All morning she'd been trembling,
waiting for Knecht Ruprecht.

So the plastic box too precious to use,
for years her prized possession,
and then the roast beef,
just as unexpected,
when she'd finally got away,
got to New York as a nanny
and people with money and children
served the thick slabs every night,
throwing away what wasn't eaten.

And then the simple fact that she's in the world at all.
She can't remember but knows better than memory
a woman—her mother—heavy on the bicycle,
peddling her slow way
through street after street
into the city, the last night of the bombing of Berlin.
She couldn't wait any longer.
At the hospital, far into delivery,
sirens emptied the rooms of every doctor, nurse, orderly,
and her mother—alone—finished the work,
picked her up and followed after
into the cavernous cellars.
For a week her parents didn't know if the other was alive.

After they'd fled Berlin's rubble,
the miracle was those coveted bananas
her father hung in the beech tree of their Rhineland home,
teasing her sister into laughter,
pretending they'd grown there—
a new fruit just for her.

He couldn't do anything
when she got beaten up
every day on the way to school,
a Protestant stranger
in a bastion of Catholicism.

Still, the bread.
Her family not yet out of Berlin, she was maybe three.
She watched her mother cut each thin slice
exactly, spread on the liverwurst,
then scrape it off so only the thinnest layer remained
and hand it to her.
No one spoke of hunger
and so she didn't think it, only how wonderful,
how perfectly delicious, to have had another slice.

Reading the Names

And I'm thinking no one could read out
all the names of the Jews the Germans killed
or all the names of the Germans who died at Stalingrad
or later—after the war—the names of all the East German women
who vanished in Siberia.

No one could read out all the names of the Vietnamese
killed.

I'm standing at the podium
by the traveling Vietnam Memorial Wall,
helping to read the names of the dead
from the thick book of them,
each of us taking our fifteen-minute turn,
so by the time the wall leaves our town,
we'll have read them all.

And because I wasn't taught phonetics
in first grade—still trying
the whole chunk of the word—
I'm stumbling over my stint in the H's.
I start to use German—
where sound matches sight—
and then I realize
it's because these are all the German Americans
falling one by one,

and a person wouldn't know
if they were the sons of Jews
or of pacifist farmers
who witnessed the Revolution.

The breeze from the Strait begins to tear
at my pages, but the names rush on

whether I can pronounce them or not,
my rolled *r* and throaty *ch* get thicker

and I'm thinking the names of the Jews *would* be German—
or Polish or French or Czech—
Germans against their own,

my hand moving the yellow card
down
to reveal the names
one by one.

I'm thinking who here could
hold properly in their mouths—gently,
accurately—the names
of the Vietnamese?

I've been told to stop at *James Herbert*
because a woman wants to read out
by herself
the name of her loved one.

I'm over a page away from him
when I feel her coming across the lawn toward me.
I can't look up from the names.
I feel her standing there crowding me.

No, it was *Hebert*, where I am right now.
She takes the card from me.
I feel my good shoes scrape on the cinder blocks
behind me.
I stumble out so she can read
the name,

but then I have to go on
reading.
Someone is holding her,

the names are coming,
why haven't I stopped to fold her
into my arms?

Why am I reading the German
names of the fallen?

They are waiting too.
They keep
forcing me forward,
to let these dead
be dead.

Blood Oranges

thinking of Lisel Mueller's poem by the same title

1.
Pretending,
nothing but the pocketbook
you'd carry on the bus

for an ordinary day of shopping,
then spirited away from Hamburg,
slipped away,

you were only fifteen
when your family
was forced out of Germany,

as if one didn't tremble
and sweat. I did,
thirty years later.

I couldn't understand
what the Germans were saying;
I couldn't get the hang

of their effortless moves
through the streets of Berlin,
giving me the slip.

I had missed *Pyrenees*
on the sixth-grade test and therefore
gained my right to them,

but I didn't know Lorca,
Dürer, Nolde,
not even Mozart,

just those few bits of German,

brokered by the Lutheran minister,
my parents living out

that American ethos
in which nothing worth knowing
exists outside God.

2.
I first ate blood oranges in Valencia,
miles and miles of orchards
outside my train window,

Franco still firmly in place.
A friend and I taking Catholic Spain
in miniskirts, neon green and orange.

Men's hands reached clear up my legs
at the top of one of Gaudi's
famous towers in Barcelona.

Breathless, winding the thousand
spiral stairs I didn't know,
men either,

though they crowded sweating
behind us, I had tumbled to it—
not everyone was rushing to see great art.

We got away that time,
laughing ourselves
to hysteria

in the warm sand of Costa Brava,
twenty and American.
We thought that could save us.

3.
We'd come south on the express,
from Germany
students and *Gastarbeiter,*

who did Germany's work,
folded *Geld* in pockets,
back to families on the weekends,

their stench and cut fruit
filling our compartment
where I couldn't sleep,

fixed on their dark
work-hardened hands
slicing a knife into oranges.

4.
Months later, the Germans
began to hear me, nodded, *yes, OK,
you're asking for oranges,*

handing them over
as if they were nothing special,
the round pocked globe of them.

I became you,
the one they sent away,
and I became your fellow Germans

who banned you,
your own split self closing
as, simply fearless,

you helped yourself to English,
a tray of tea cakes,
yes, please.

5.
Neither of us knew
we were putting on the other,
I falling in love

with all the things
which stood for your exile,
Hamburg, Brötchen, Wald, und See,

while you married your American husband
and calmly let yourself watch
the carving of Germany.

By now this far along the other's path
we sit here tonight
in your tiny apartment kitchen,

eating blueberries and milk
giving some sentences so easily to one language,
some to the other,

I can see us hunched in the bushes
near the border,
hastily trading dresses, shoes, coats

straightening collars,
in the last minute, buttons,
and then

entering the other
country with that great gift—
disguised and accepted.